Southern Living.
QUICK
DECORATING

Southern Living.
QUICK
DECORATING

From
The Homes Editors of
Southern Living

Text by
Julia Hamilton Thomason

Library of Congress Catalog Number: 93-87429
Hardcover ISBN: 0-8487-1143-2
Softcover ISBN: 0-8487-1416-4
Manufactured in the United States of America

Fourth Printing 2000

Editor-in-Chief: Nancy J. Fitzpatrick
Senior Homes Editor: Mary Kay Culpepper
Senior Editor, Editorial Services: Olivia Kindig Wells
Director of Manufacturing: Jerry Higdon
Art Director: James Boone

Quick Decorating
Editor: Rebecca Brennan
Editorial Assistant: Janica Lynn York
Designer: Melissa Jones Clark
Copy Editor: L. Amanda Owens
Copy Assistant: Leslee Rester Johnson
Production Manager: Rick Litton
Associate Production Manager: Theresa L. Beste
Production Assistant: Marianne Jordan
Assistant Art Director: Cynthia R. Cooper
Illustrator: Anita S. Bice
Senior Production Designer: Larry Hunter
Publishing Systems Administrator: Rick Tucker

CONTENTS

Let The People Who
Know Give You The Confidence
To Master Quick Decorating.

Foreword

Dear Friends,

Many years ago, when I was new to *Southern Living*, I bought my first house. It was a bungalow so small that it looked as if a hermit crab lived inside. The previous owners had covered up the windows, carpeted the hardwood floors, and painted the molding and walls all the same color. When I moved in, I set about making it brighter. After a while—and a whole lot of work—it began to look like home.

About that time, a young woman from Mississippi joined the staff as projects editor of *Southern Living*. She was Julia Hamilton Thomason. I thought she had a keen eye for color and design, but I didn't know for certain until she visited my home and, as a favor I'll always remember, rearranged my living room. Her changes transformed it. Today, she is still transforming, encouraging our readers with great ideas and simple projects that just about any of us can do quickly and inexpensively.

In this book, Julia writes about putting the finishing touches to any room in your home without the expense of a decorator and without the do-it-yourself look. Here are gorgeous, affordable ideas presented in a simple, direct, how-to format.

Quick Decorating starts with profiles of people who, like Julia, really understand the concept. The rest of it is organized around the times you will need to pull a look together quickly. When you move in, when you've got the weekend for a make-over, when guests are at the door, or when you just want a change—that's when you'll reach for this book. For my first home, it would have been a lifesaver.

I like to think of this book as the best of *Southern Living* with Julia Thomason's special touch. Here Julia tells how you can enjoy living in a home that expresses your own personal style, just as she does every month in the pages of *Southern Living*.

Best regards,
John Alex Floyd, Jr., Editor
Southern Living

Quick Decorating:

Hocus-Pocus Quick decorating may seem like magic. Its wizardry, however, is easy to explain. And, fortunately, **easy to duplicate.** Who has all the secrets? Well, this quartet of experts will teach you **how to create** your own enchantment. Robert

Chesnut's place in the sun comes about in a **casual, color-filled** flash, thanks to his alchemy with paint, fabric, and a few found treasures.

It's An Attitude

A classicist at heart, Philip Morris conjures up **a fast twist** on tradition. Cathy Chapman charms with her free-spirited ways, enhancing carefully placed family pieces with a changing collection of **lucky finds.** And at Christmas (when everyone wants to **decorate quickly**), Kreis Beall bewitches her farmhouse with naturally wonderful decorations. What's the magic word? **Inspiration.** And it's right here.

Carolina Charm

This quick-thinking couple splashed garage sale finds with paint and brightened old furnishings with fabric. Their fresh approach to quick decorating is cheerful, casual, and full of ideas.

A Carefree Style Robert and Suzanne Chesnut remodeled a fifty-year-old beach house—twice. After working on the house for most of one summer, damage from Hurricane Hugo made it necessary for them to start all over again in the fall. Decorating the second time around, the Chesnuts (with daughter, Blair) implemented a variety of techniques to turn all kinds of furniture into decorating treasures. A potpourri of pine, bamboo, and wicker pieces gives their seaside cottage a breezy, hospitable feel.

A Colorful Approach The Chesnuts painted, sponged, and stippled inexpensive furniture to add new life and color to their home. They painted walls bright white and tinted the ceilings with pastel colors that echo the fabrics they chose for the furnishings.

Other quick studies: Ready-made gingham tablecloths become table skirts, pillow covers, and bedspreads; casual accessories such as wooden sculptures, straw baskets, and birdhouses add to the lighthearted atmosphere.

The warm pine hutch offers both practical and decorative storage for china, table linens, and other household items the Chesnuts use every day.

Island Flair

A whimsical painting, full of color and life, sets the palette for the stripes, checks, and florals that cover the furniture. Suzanne and Robert composed an arrangement of old bottles and shells on the mantel that speaks of the sea just beyond the cottage.

The summery blue-and-white scheme, animated by shades of rose and raspberry, unifies the couple's assortment of hand-me-down and vintage furniture.

Color is always the quickest way to dress up a room, and the Chesnuts applied it swiftly and evenhandedly almost everywhere. Wicker chairs that Robert inherited were drenched in white paint and softened with colorful floral cushions. The couple revived old tabletops by spattering them with blue and white paint. And they brightened the summer-darkened fireplace with a big container of fresh flowers set atop a painted stool.

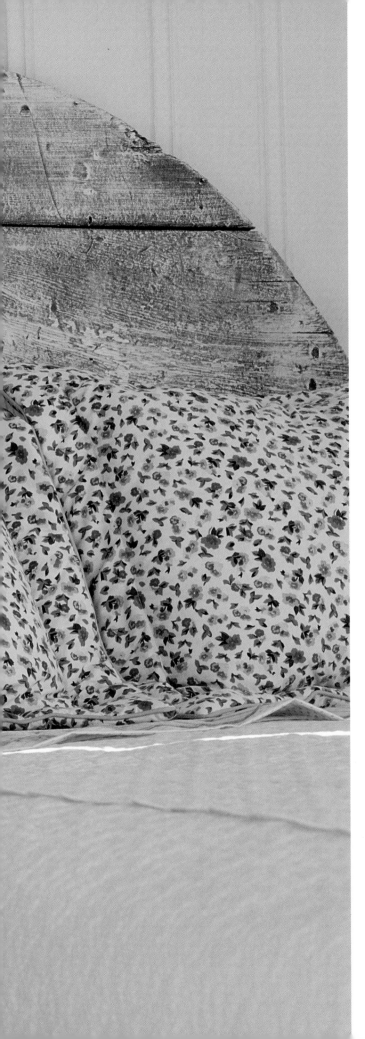

New Life For Old Treasures

One of the couple's favorite projects was the headboard in the guest bedroom. Suzanne and Robert appropriated the top of an old round picnic table that had washed ashore after Hurricane Hugo. They cut the table-top in half, sponged one piece with white paint, and situated it behind the guest bed. It is the perfect size and adds weathered texture to the room.

The Chesnuts also revitalized several flea market tables and chairs with bright blue paint and added a few well-placed accents in white.

Form And Function

This editor travels extensively while researching
articles on architecture and urban planning. His Alabama home
speaks volumes about good, fast design.

Refined Lines Architecture is one of
Philip Morris's consuming interests, and
he makes it a visual theme at home. The
clean, polished background his rooms
offer can give even the most casual decorator some classic ideas.

For instance, he added a wall of bookshelves
that allows the dining room to function as a comfortable library—a great way to maximize the
purpose of a room that's not in constant use. (If
you don't want to remodel, use purchased book-
case units in lieu of built-ins.)

Philip chose furnishings that work
for dining and reading. A nineteenth-
century oak refectory table and a scale-
down pair of upholstered armchairs are
ideal for this double duty.

The notion of getting two rooms out
of one is typical of Philip's style. So is his ability
to explore an assortment of furnishing resources.
Philip scopes out the offerings at places like hardware shops and craft galleries. And when he can-
not find what he wants at retail, he commissions
an original work from an artist or craftsperson.

An Entertaining Kitchen Instead of using a conventional kitchen island, Philip's inventiveness led him to a garden shop where he bought a square column and then topped it with a round of black marble. The table is convenient for quick meals or for serving wine and cheese to friends.

The tabletop is just one of the black accents that punctuate Philip's neutral color scheme. For the kitchen, he found a classical column lamp with a flared black shade. Placed so that it is visible from the dining room, the lamp adds a note of formality in tune with the pieces in adjacent rooms.

High stools with black-lacquer frames provide handy seating and repeat the color. Oriental rugs, a surprise in the kitchen, add sparks of crimson and claret, reinforcing Philip's crisp design scheme.

Quick-Change Artistry Philip liked the off-white color of his living room chairs, but he was ready for a softer look. His solution—a fabric throw—is an idea anyone can use to change the style, the lines, or even the color of armless chairs. The throws are easily removed for dry cleaning or storage.

How he did it: Philip placed a sheet over one of the chairs, pinned the loose fabric to fit as he wanted, and then had a seamstress use the sheet as a pattern for making the throws. Because of the thick welting sewn to the bottom edges, the fabric of the finished covers falls into graceful folds.

In this sunny corner, Philip proudly displays what appears to be an antique map of Rome. In truth, it's a reproduction. He glued the inexpensive print to heavy cardboard and framed it simply. The map is an important focal point at the end of the room, and it always reminds Philip of one of his favorite cities.

Rapid-Fire Style On A Budget

Antiques and classics are the backbone of this designer's Texas home. With this foundation of quality, she combines flea market and thrift store finds for an interesting mix.

Comfort And Personality Interior designer Cathy Chapman likes to decorate with furniture and artwork obtained over time, filling in with constantly changing new acquisitions.

The home that she shares with her husband, Paul, and two young sons shows how she does it. Cathy relaxes the formality of family pieces and collected antiques with high-impact objects such as a glass-topped coffee table and a cowhide rug.

Pulling It Together One of the strongest focal points in the small living room is Paul's collection of photographs. To unify the group, Cathy matted and framed them simply and identically. While these prints are the work of the famous photographer Jacques-Henri Lartique, any black and whites—even your own masterpieces—will do. Hung in an orderly grid, snapshots lend interest to a room.

Part of the reason the photographs look great is the neutral wall color. It doesn't compete with them for attention.

To keep this room full of classic furniture from looking as if all the pieces were purchased at the same time, Cathy adds subtle interest with up-to-date accents such as the sleek black lamp—a bit of contemporary sculpture in her largely traditional room.

Something else that brings a bit of energy: Cathy's lively tabletop arrangements. She teams the colorful with the original when she slips red tapers into her picturesque cactus candlesticks. And she often works flowers, books, and pieces from her pottery collection into these compositions.

Traditional And Contemporary

Still lifes make more of an impact, Cathy says, if they mean something to you. A folk-art armadillo and a vase of yellow roses sit side by side on the buffet to remind Cathy of her Texas roots.

Cathy is particularly adept at combining diverse elements. In the dining room, conventionally styled chairs that Paul inherited pair with a clean-lined glass-and-iron dining table. The glass top doesn't visually crowd the room the way a wooden tabletop might. Overhead, the wrought iron Mexican chandelier has a contemporary look, even though Cathy found it in her grandmother's attic.

The black-and-silver framed Irish mirror was a lucky thrift store find; it is versatile enough to relocate to another room as her collection of accessories grows.

Holiday Spin

Kreis Beall's Tennessee farmhouse is nestled in a fold of the Great Smoky Mountains. Its country comfort provides a warm backdrop for quick and easy Christmas decorations brought in from the great outdoors.

Natural Wonders Kreis and her husband, Sandy, let the rustic atmosphere of their farmhouse suggest a style of Christmas decorating that is as fresh as nature itself.

Their secret is the generous use of readily available materials, such as greenery, fruit, flowers, and spices. This tactic results in simple but luxurious flourishes that welcome celebration. Two glorious examples: the boxwood garlands festooning the dining room and the pine coffee table laden with oranges, apples, and winter roses (overleaf).

Bright Ideas Kreis nestles most of her holiday groupings in natural materials. For example, a birdhouse village, springing up from a bed of moss and dried flowers, spreads out along the top of a pine dresser in the family room.

Kreis grows and dries flowers throughout the year to decorate her home at Christmastime. She fills in with fresh miniature roses that are easily found in winter at a florist's shop. And she buys her favorite materials—citrus and apples, aromatic spices, and flower bulbs—in bulk at considerable savings.

Fragrant Accents Long before the holidays, Kreis plants narcissus bulbs in clay pots to bloom in time for Christmas. She then sprinkles quick-sprouting rye grass seed onto the soil. When everything grows, the pots look like miniature gardens. She places them on tables and in windows all around the house.

The natural theme continues in the bedroom where lengths of dried vine are tied across the bedposts for the effect of a homespun canopy.

A romantic arch of dried flowers tops the window.

Throughout the farmhouse, Kreis uses yellow flowers, fabrics, and fruit as accents: Underneath the banister in the living room, she drapes a table with a yellow-and-white quilt and banks it with pots of flowers. White crockery bowls are heaped with fresh fruit, presents are wrapped with gold-dusted ribbon, and the entire setting gleams in the warmth of votive candles.

When You

Ready, Set, Go
Where do you
begin after the
moving van
pulls away? Quick decorating gives
you a **head start** on loving your new
place—well before you've sent the
last empty box to the recycling
center. Start by **stenciling** some
curtains to cover the windows. Let the linens

First Move In

do all the work in your bedroom, coordinating everything from dust ruffles to seat cushions. **Get the most** out of the furniture you already have with **new ideas** for your old arrangements. Once the **basics are done,** move on to the details that signal your personal style. Go ahead:

Organize the bookshelves. Set out **your treasures.** Hang those pictures. Before you know it, your new place will feel **just like home.**

Breezy, Easy

Suitable For Hanging Nothing makes you feel settled in a new house as quickly as well-dressed windows. For an imaginative yet inexpensive way to fancy them up, stencil purchased sheer curtains. Adapt patterns from your room's fabrics or wallpaper for a perfect match.

Clear Cuts To make a stencil, you will need sheets of clear acetate, an indelible marker, craft knife, permanent fabric paints, masking tape, and stencil brush (all available at crafts stores). Place an acetate sheet on fabric or wallpaper and use the marker to trace the most distinctive shapes. Put the stencil on a cutting surface. With a craft knife, cut away the acetate inside the shapes.

Color Play Next, select your colors. Washable, permanent fabric paints are available in a rainbow of shades. If you plan to stencil your curtains with an overall pattern of small shapes such as leaves or diamonds, consider using white paint on white fabric; a contrasting shade may look spotty at a distance.

To keep the work area clean, tape a plastic trash bag over the surface and then place the curtain panel on top. Tape the stencil to the fabric. Place a small amount of paint on an old plate or disposable pie pan. Dip the stencil brush into the paint and dab the paint onto the fabric. When the paint is nearly dry, remove the stencil and clean the paint from the reverse side. When the painted fabric is completely dry, reposition the stencil and continue painting.

A Well-Planned Scheme
Color-coordinated sheets and linens provide the quickest route to bedroom harmony. Solids, stripes, and prints that share a complementary range effortlessly introduce color into the room and set the tone for decorative accessories.

Pillow covers become a fast finish in the time it takes to slip them on. In this room, clever edging treatments add layered detail. On the large shams, for example, strips of solid and print fabrics were sewn together lengthwise and then gathered to make wide ruffles.

Layering also ennobles an otherwise humble particleboard table, which becomes a decorating asset when covered with a solid peach cotton skirt and topped with a lively striped overlay.

Large windows are wonderful, yet in a bedroom they may need to be covered for privacy. Here, lacy curtains screen the view without blocking the sunshine. They are framed by floral print panels that have been topped with a simple, straight valance. Rosettes at the valance corners soften the intersection of strong vertical and horizontal lines.

Accessorizing—the very thing that makes a house look lived in—may seem daunting, but it can be easy. Rely on interesting things you already have. In a bedroom, consider the charm of items such as toy animals and dolls. These sentimental treasures make your room even more special. Hats, hatboxes, and dried flowers also help to provide a finishing touch to a room without a lot of expense.

Small Is Beautiful
In tiny rooms, little negatives add up in a big way. Chances are that if your home is more than a dozen years old, your bathrooms may have some out-of-date features. These before-and-after photos show how easy it is to give a bath a completely new look by replacing a few key elements.

Glittering Specifics
Adding brass fixtures gives a humdrum vanity instant status, and painting the cabinet freshens the finish. Wall sconces fitted with parchment shades replace ordinary light fixtures and bring a touch of refinement. A wood-framed medicine cabinet mirror is functional and handsome. Search antiques shops and furniture stores for one that's the perfect reflection of your good taste.

Glamorize the Bath

New Introductions
Any one of these changes can give the littlest room a big lift: Freshen existing wallpaper with a vivid border. Or splurge on a rich wallpaper to really dress things up. To hide unsightly pipes, attach a skirt with Velcro to the edge of a sink.

Finally, consider introducing accessories ordinarily reserved for other rooms of the house, such as small lamps or botanical prints—even chairs or tables, if you have the space.

Garden

In The Fold For rooms where you need extra seating but don't have lots of space, use metal furniture to add alfresco flair. The spare lines of this folding French park chair allow it to fit in easily with the whitewashed country bench. This is a perfect pairing for a sun-room or screened porch.

Metal Urge Sidled up to a table, simple metal chairs contribute neoclassic style. A canvas tablecloth and weathered statue bolster the garden mood. The unobtrusive lines of the chairs allow them to blend with almost any decor.

Style

Great Outdoors This black
wrought-iron garden arm-
chair has an airy appeal that
makes it a natural outdoors.
A cotton seat cushion gives
some softness to its angular
lines, yet allows the lattice-
work chair back to show. In
a display of versatility, the
cushioned ottoman doubles
as an impromptu table.

Inside Move When the
weather turns cool, bring the
same chair and ottoman
indoors. Relax their hard
look with comfortable
printed linen cushions. For
well-designed outdoor pieces,
check furniture stores and
garden catalogs.

Set In Concrete

Harvest new ideas for quick-and-easy end tables and coffee tables from garden pots and statuary. Small concrete figures such as these rakish rabbits make unique sculptural bases and will bring an outdoor freshness inside. A sturdy terra-cotta pot or planter—particularly one that boasts a distinctive shape—creates a stylish table when topped with marble or glass. For fun, fill a pot or planter with a collection of pinecones or seashells to view through a glass top.

Old Things, New Ways

Many homes have an awkward corner, a gaping spot under a window, or an extra bit of floor space that presents a decorating challenge.

An eclectic approach to filling these holes offers great potential for creative arrangement and display. An unexpected mix of furniture and accessories is a fun way to add your personal stamp while solving your decorating dilemmas with ease.

For example, use a rug, shawl, or tapestry instead of a conventional tablecloth to add interesting texture and character. Paint the walls in vibrant jewel tones to give instant impact to unexceptional rooms. Strong colors also provide a dramatic backdrop for sculptural groupings of long bare twigs that become focal points for the tops of tables and bookcases.

Create a conservatory ambience in an odd corner by clustering garden pedestals and containers of plants. Pair rustic furniture with more refined accessories to spark individuality.

QUICK IDEA

Contain Yourself Both old and new containers, including planters, watering cans, crocks, and clay pots, are great for displaying plants and arrangements of flowers and foliage. Buy vases and containers you like when they are at the right price, even if you don't have an immediate location in mind. Look for pieces that can be used in more than one way. When you get home, rearrange, readjust, and reinvent.

Under And Over Does a piece of furniture seem too small or too leggy once you've placed it? Put something above it or below it and change the scale for the better.

Go underneath a console table for convenient storage and display of magazines, photograph albums, and stacks of books. Or fill the space with a wicker basket piled with dried flowers to add color in a charming way.

The surface of a table or chest is the perfect setting for groupings of framed photographs, porcelain pieces, and handsome old books. By placing a tall painting, mirror, or tray on top, you can expand the furniture's visual height—and make it fit in perfectly.

Making Other Arrangements

Display's The Thing Being flexible in the way you set out your favorite possessions is the easiest way to achieve a look of your own.

It may sound obvious, but bookshelves aren't just for books. They also allow you space to parade your collections and personal mementos.

Think of what you can do to give your bookshelves impact: Paint the back wall a vivid shade; when the shelves are filled, you'll catch glimpses of drama here and there. Place a small lamp on a shelf to add a warm glow. Position an overstuffed chair and a good reading light close by, and you've created a practical library area.

Don't feel that you have to keep everything you own on display at all times. Try rotating and storing accessories to keep your home's decor fresh. Let the seasons set the stage. For example, bring out brass candlesticks in winter and glass ones in summer.

Experiment by putting out a mix of the things you like.

Couple antique treasures with new finds and vary textures and materials. Combine porcelain, iron, and wooden plates in a single grouping.

Sitting on a bookshelf or stacked on a sideboard, objects look better when they are set on a base. Pile old leather-bound volumes or antique wooden boxes to make a pedestal for a contemporary bowl or sculpture. You'll be surprised how important even a modest piece will look.

Consider showcasing posters or prints within your shelves. Later, you can move your art around so you'll continue to view it anew.

Then again, you might want to camouflage a too familiar picture. Arrange flowers, books, or pottery in front of it and use it as a pattern-filled backdrop.

Don't worry if your treasures seem too diverse. Remember, because you are the curator of your own collections, they will always work together.

On The Shelf When shelves are interestingly arranged, guests will be drawn to them to admire their contents. The cardinal rule: the best-looking bookshelves appear to be well filled. But in case you don't have enough items for all the shelves in your home, here's how to make a few good things go a long way.

True Grid If your shelves are adjustable, arrange them to form an eye-pleasing grid with the deepest spaces placed nearest the floor to give visual support for shelves above. The remaining spaces should become progressively smaller.

Book Values Vary the arrangement of your books. Place some books vertically; stack others horizontally to serve as bookends and as bases for small decorative objects. Lean a few picture books against the back wall to show off attractive covers. Feature a favorite novel by standing it upright.

Gallery Openings As you position books on shelves, leave openings for artwork and photographs. Hang a small painting on the wall behind the shelves or place a large one on a stand or easel. Arrange your photographs with other personal mementos, setting them near eye level for easier viewing.

Fine Points Use accessories to unify color and scale. Notice how the pieces of blue-and-white porcelain echo two of the colors in the upholstered chair. A quartet of brass candlesticks warms the framed architectural illustration.

The Angle On Art What's the quickest, most relaxed way to display your photographs, paintings, and drawings? Set them on a tabletop and lean them against the wall. By placing your pieces at table height, you instantly make them easier to see. Adding other pieces—vases, trays, lamps, and the like—gives you the chance to create an impromptu tableau.

Select a theme for your display and then group whatever you have collected. Vary the arrangement of the pieces until you achieve a pleasing composition.

The overall effect is usually more successful if you work with more than one painting, print, or photograph as the focus of the arrangement. Remember the "Rule of Three": A trio of similar items of different heights and sizes works especially well; five or more can be too many.

Smart Art

Smart Art The right artwork can strengthen the design of any room. If you want it to be the focal point—the effect created by the large oil painting shown at right—one of your best bets is to scour student art shows for overscaled pieces at reasonable prices. Alternatively, look for oversized exhibition posters from museum shops.

Pictorial calendars and bargain-priced art books are good sources of inexpensive prints to mat and frame as sets. For variety, stack prints, one above the other, to fill the wall with a grid. Or arrange a series in a row to create the effect of a frieze.

Quick Thinking

Starting a home? Make it look like you've been there for ages. Cover bare walls, soften the windows, and brighten a few blank corners with these speedy ideas.

The Latest Word The Victorians often read five or six books simultaneously, stacking the ones they were currently reading close at hand. Take a page from their book and put yours on display, piling them in a seldom-used side chair. Stagger dark and light spines in the stack for visual interest.

Heavy Metal A wire basket—the sort that is often hung on a garden wall—makes a great "clutter" holder in the kitchen, and it's a pretty container for extra hand towels and soaps in the powder room.

Nice Spice Add a soupçon of color to your kitchen by framing a cotton damask towel. The handsome pictorial designs are woven in a variety of colors particularly appropriate to kitchens and breakfast rooms. Or frame a figured cotton lace panel mounted atop a tinted mat.

Crowning Touch With two simple steps, a lace-bordered tablecloth becomes a swift swag. First, center the tablecloth on a wooden curtain rod and thumbtack the cloth to the edges of the rod. Second, gather the fabric and hide the tacks with ribbon bows.

Youthful Antics Artwork is seldom a priority in a new home budget. If your child's a budding artist, though, show off those drawings in your living room. Simulate a frame with a piece of black posterboard. Attach the drawing to the board with colorful plastic paper clips and set it on a small easel. Exhibit other art projects with the picture for a proud-parent vignette.

When You've

Saturday And Sunday Those two little days are rife with big possibilities for quick decorating. A weekend is **all it takes** to complete each of the projects in this chapter. **Change** the character of your walls. Make

a **statement** with some eloquent pillows. Rediscover the old-fashioned art of decoupage. **Paint** a floorcloth. Spray some spunk on an area rug.

Got A Weekend

Master the art of faux verdigris and make your friends green with envy. **Teach** an old lampshade new tricks. Turn a tray **into a table**. Make your sideboard take center stage with a fabric screen. Create a **center-of-attention** ottoman. With each of these endeavors, **time** is of the essence. So **get busy**. If you start now, when Monday morning rolls around, you'll be **living it up** with a great new look.

Play Around With Paint

Splash And Dash These decorative finishes turn plain walls into dramatic backdrops in just a few easy steps. The red wall shown here is sponged, and the blue wall is ragged.

With these simple techniques, you'll use two shades of the same color. The first coat is light-colored paint; the second is a glaze coat, a translucent mixture of dark paint and glazing liquid that's the key to professional-looking results.

With either sponging or ragging, practice first on a piece of wallboard to make sure you get the procedure down pat.

Sponging At a paint store, choose a color card that shows one color in a range of values from light to dark. Pick the base coat (latex paint in satin or semigloss) from the lighter colors. From the same card, select a darker shade of oil-based paint to mix with the glazing liquid. You will also need painter's tape, glazing liquid, acrylic latex varnish in a satin or semigloss finish, paint thinner, a foam paint roller, foam brush, natural sponge, and paintbrushes.

Tape the ceiling, window frames, and edges of the trim with painter's tape to protect them from

base paint and glaze. Paint the base coat with a foam roller and use a foam brush for corners and edges. Dry overnight.

Make the glaze coat from approximately one-quarter dark oil-based paint and three-quarters glazing liquid. The more glazing liquid and the less paint in the mixture, the more translucent the look will be. If the glaze coat is too thick to apply, add a few drops of paint thinner.

Dip a natural sponge in the glaze coat and lightly dab it on the wall, working in three-foot-square sections. Slightly overlap sections and use a clean paintbrush to blend in edges and corners. Apply paint lightly—you can always go back and add another sponged layer. When dry, cover walls with two coats of acrylic latex varnish.

Ragging Follow the steps for sponging up to the application of the glaze coat.

Brush on the glaze coat, covering a section about three-foot square. Wad a cotton rag and press it with a rolling motion into the damp glaze coat, creating texture. Brush the glaze coat on the next section, overlapping to blend edges. Use a fresh rag to create texture as before. Work quickly to keep a wet edge.

Allow walls to dry completely. Seal the finish by applying two coats of acrylic latex varnish.

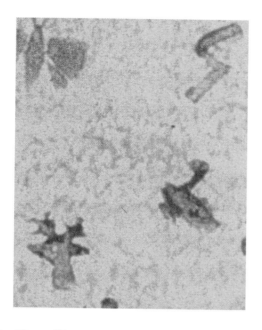

Make Your Stamp
Potato prints—always a favorite with kids—brighten plain walls with folk-art patterns.

The technique is child's play. First, paint your walls a strong color, such as this brilliant yellow. Cut several large potatoes in half and carve a simple motif—a leaf, star, or crescent moon—in each one. Then dip the cut ends of the potato halves in contrasting colors of latex paint and stamp on the patterns. To get the best results, experiment first on a practice board.

For a wainscot, paint the walls below the chair rail a color that will contrast with the upper portion. Then potato-stamp the designs below the chair rail.

To protect your paintwork, seal the walls with varnish. For a mellow, aged look, you can hand-tint the varnish with pigments from the paint store.

A Brush With Glory

Fanciful Fabrics Having trouble finding just the right fabrics? Then paint your own. Your original designs will be durable, washable, and sun-resistant on fabrics decorated with permanent fabric paints.

The materials you'll need: permanent fabric paints, colorless extender, brushes, and masking tape. Kitchen sponges cut into geometric shapes with a craft knife come in handy for stamping.

Playful Detail Effervescent effects are easy to come by. To make stripes on fabric, apply masking tape to areas you want to remain white; then dip a sponge into the paint mixture and dab it onto the fabric. Peel the masking tape off after the paint is dry. A square sponge is useful for making a checkerboard effect. And an inch-wide brush is just the thing for row upon row of squiggles and curlicues.

Choose The Fabric

For slipcovers and pillows, use untreated all-cotton canvas. For bed linens, consider using cotton or cotton blend fabrics. Pre-wash to remove any sizing that might interfere with the way the paint adheres.

As with all slipcovers, it's important to be able to easily clean the fabric. Test the durability of the paint by washing a painted scrap of fabric, and you'll know what to expect when laundering the finished sheets or slipcovers.

Select The Paint

You can mix your own fabric paints or select from the wide variety of premixed colors available in art supply and crafts stores. For a light look, use three parts of colorless extender mixed with one part of paint.

Be sure to mix enough paint to finish the entire project. Use small glass jars or airtight plastic food containers to keep the paint workable.

Begin The Design

Bed linens and smaller pieces are easier to paint flat on a big table. For slipcovers, it's best to work directly on the piece of furniture so that you can see where the pattern falls. To keep paint from seeping through the fabric, use a layer of thin plastic painter's drape under the slipcover, molding it to fit the piece.

Getting Specific Vary the shape and texture of your sponge to put personality in your painted patterns. A basket-weave pattern is formed with a corrugated sponge dipped in paint and applied at alternating right angles. Stylized flowers can be made with a doughnut-shaped sponge.

The Brush-Off Three pinwheel brush strokes instantly form another kind of flower. The spacing establishes the overall scale and repeat of the pattern. Stand back from your painted fabric occasionally to evaluate the overall effect. Let paint dry before you add more.

Deep Background Leaving some of the background unpainted for contrast, decorate the fabric with three different patterns: larger and smaller leaf shapes and triangular petals. If you inadvertently smudge the paint, don't worry. Minor mistakes only add character.

The Big Finish Paint crescent strokes to make the flower design really pop. And for the final step, make dots for the flower centers.

When you're all through, treat your painted designs with a coat of stain-resistant spray. It'll keep them looking fresh longer.

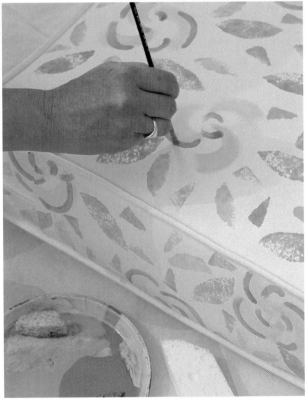

Paper Trails

Table Grace This elegant garden-room table looks like a hand-painted original, but it's simply a metal table given new status with a delightful decoupage design.

Where to find the pictures? Check out calendars, wrapping paper, wallpaper, and sale-table books.

Before You Start After you've cut out the designs you want to use, make a few trial arrangements until you are satisfied with the results. To protect the cutouts, place them face up on newspaper and apply several light coats of clear acrylic spray, letting each coat dry before spraying on the next.

Spray The Glue Spread a stack of newspaper to protect your work surface. Place a single cutout, printed side down, on the newspaper and heavy-duty spray adhesive (available at art supply stores) on the back of the cutout. Remove the cutout and discard the top layer of newspaper to avoid getting adhesive on the next cutout. Handle each cutout carefully to keep the adhesive from smudging the table surface.

Finish Your Masterpiece Put a cutout on the surface and press it firmly into place. Continue gluing one piece at a time, overlapping edges if desired. Finish with several coats of quick-drying clear spray lacquer. Protect the decorated surface with a piece of glass cut to the same dimensions as your tabletop.

A Dishy Idea These stylish plates, with the pricey look of hand-painted porcelain, are almost too easy to make. Underneath their chic exteriors are inexpensive clear glass plates embellished with colorful paper cutouts. Display them as you would any great china collection—atop plate stands or decoratively arranged on the wall.

Select A Motif Clip an illustration from a magazine, cut out a design from wrapping paper, or use a precut decoupage motif. Spread a stack of newspaper to protect your work surface. Brush a thin layer of clear-drying craft glue onto the printed side of the cutout and place it, printed side down, on the underside of a plate. Rub the cutout with a spoon to flatten.

Make Your Mark Use a damp paper towel to remove any glue smudges. When the glue is dry, embellish with a metallic oil paint marker available at crafts stores. Using a ruler as a guide, outline the cutout and add highlights to the bottom and edges of the plate.

Final Color For background interest, apply spray paint to the underside of the plate. You can mist a single solid color onto the plate or create a spattered effect by slightly depressing the button on the can of spray paint. For a dappled look, just spray several colors, applying them one at a time.

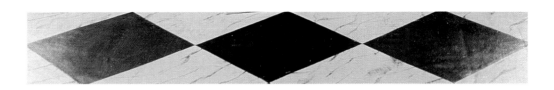

Something Underfoot

Art For The Floor Two hundred years ago, Americans favored floorcloths—hand-painted canvas rugs—as a stylish yet inexpensive way to warm their homes. They're popular again today because they still sport the same virtues.

Once you buy a preprimed canvas at an art supply store, the most challenging aspect of making a floorcloth is settling on a design and a color scheme. Two classic patterns, diamonds (made easily with masking tape) and fleurs-de-lis, work in rooms that range from country to contemporary. As for colors, just choose from the ones in your fabrics and furnishings, and you'll have the beginnings of a fine work of art.

Making A Floorcloth For a 4- by 6-foot floor-cloth, you will need: a 52- by 76-inch No. 10 preprimed artist's canvas, drop cloth, paint roller, two or three shades of latex wall paint, stencil (optional), yardstick, drafting tape, paintbrushes, varnish, and hot-glue gun and glue sticks.

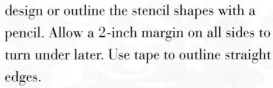

Spread the canvas on the drop cloth. With the paint roller, apply the latex paint background to the preprimed surface of the canvas. When the paint has dried, lightly draw the floorcloth

design or outline the stencil shapes with a pencil. Allow a 2-inch margin on all sides to turn under later. Use tape to outline straight edges.

With a paintbrush, fill in the large blocks first; paint within the stencil outlines last. Let dry. Remove any tape.

Apply three coats of varnish with the paint roller, following manu-facturer's instructions. Fold under 2 inches on each side of the canvas and secure using the hot-glue gun.

Spray On The Personality

Coir rugs, woven of fibers taken from coconut shells, are beautiful, economic floor coverings with almost unlimited potential. You can make a good thing even better by giving your coir rug a border of color. Just use masking tape to block off the pattern and after a few coats of enamel spray paint, you'll have a customized design that coordinates with your room.

Home furnishing catalogs are a good source of coir rugs in a variety of sizes and colors. For this project, you'll also need: scissors, a yardstick, masking tape, and spray paint. You may find it helpful to spread out the rug in the room where you're planning to use it and then try to visualize how it will look when completed. You may want to experiment with spray paint on the back of the rug. Use light coats that won't show through.

Keep in mind that manufacturers recommend a rug pad to prevent dyes added to these natural fibers from transferring to the floor. For the same reason, these rugs should not be placed on carpeting—they could bleed through. One more consideration: the natural colors in these rugs are not waterproof and may fade in sunlight.

Painting A Natural-Fiber Rug

Use 1½- and 2-inch-wide masking tape. Tape over areas that are to stay the original color and paint the untaped areas.

To create squares, make two parallel rows, 1 inch apart, with tape. Insert small pieces of tape at right angles between the parallel rows.

To make a painted band at the edges of the rug, apply two rows of tape alongside each other and then remove the outer row.

Cover the center of the rug with posterboard or newspaper, and tape to secure. Paint the rug with spray enamel, working carefully to gradually build up the color. Let dry completely before removing the tape and newspaper or posterboard.

Lights Fantastic

Wearin' O' The Green A painted verdigris finish adds the rustic look of weathered copper to even the most mundane metal lamp. This one benefits as well from a new footed base, brassy finial, and snappy black shade.

To begin the transformation, sand the lamp base and then prime it with white-pigmented shellac. Let dry.

Apply one coat of black latex using a sponge brush. When dry, dab on an uneven coat of blue-green latex, wiping on the paint in vertical streaks with a slightly dry sponge. Allow half of the black to show through.

Add highlights of gold paint to rims and outer curves. To finish, use a natural sponge to apply a light topcoat of pale green, leaving about a quarter of the undercoats showing through; smear this coat of paint slightly with a sponge brush. Let dry.

Brighten The Shade
The crisp, tailored flourish of a fabric-covered lampshade can illuminate your home with style. Wrapping an ordinary parchment or linen shade with fabric is a classic finishing touch—it looks good, and it's easy.

The critical component, a multipurpose spray adhesive, stays tacky for about fifteen minutes. You'll have plenty of time to adjust the fabric on the shade. In addition to the fabric and the adhesive spray, you'll need scissors, a single-edge razor blade, and fabric glue. Because the print will be running on the diagonal by the time it wraps to the back seam, fabrics with a nondirectional pattern work best.

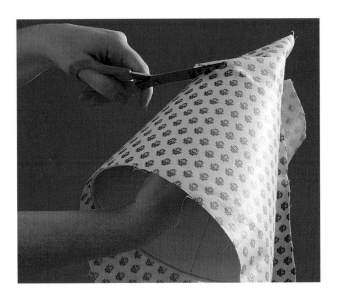

Stick The Fabric
Choose a sturdy fabric and place it around the lampshade to get the approximate amount you'll need. Cut the fabric to fit. Spray the shade with adhesive. Smooth and position the fabric in place.

Trim close to the top and bottom rims of the shade with scissors. With the razor blade, trim the remaining excess fabric in a straight line at the back.

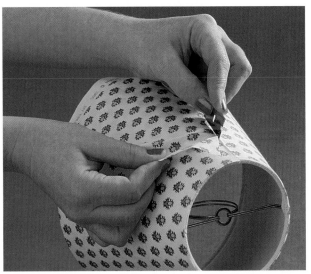

Trim And Fit
You can edge the shade with decorative braid or double-fold bias tape. Alternatively, you can use the same fabric as the lamp. To make the edging shown here, cut two 1¾-inch-wide bias (diagonal) strips, one long enough to cover the shade's top rim and the other for the bottom rim. Fold the long edges of each strip toward the center and press. Fold the strip in half and press again. Center the fold along the rim of the shade and secure each strip with fabric glue.

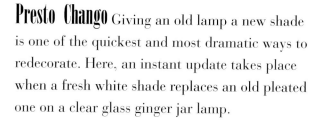

Presto Chango Giving an old lamp a new shade is one of the quickest and most dramatic ways to redecorate. Here, an instant update takes place when a fresh white shade replaces an old pleated one on a clear glass ginger jar lamp.

New Shapes A white Empire-style shade transforms an outdated lamp into one that's more fashionable. (White shades reflect the maximum amount of light, while ecru shades cast a softer glow.) A new finial tops the lamp.

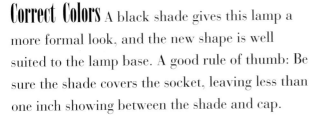

Correct Colors A black shade gives this lamp a more formal look, and the new shape is well suited to the lamp base. A good rule of thumb: Be sure the shade covers the socket, leaving less than one inch showing between the shade and cap.

Enhance Features Replacing a too narrow burlap shade with a graceful hexagonal one showcases the "candles" of this floor lamp. To make sure you find the perfect shade, take the lamp with you to the store.

Quick

Tray Magnifique Placing a decorative tray on a base is a great way to create a quick end table or coffee table. This tole gallery tray is set on a handcrafted iron base. A vintage wooden crate atop the same base would render a more relaxed look.

Home Bases A traditional luggage rack makes a fast foundation for a large tray such as this antique one. Choose a rack with a dark finish to link the table to the traditional furnishings in the room. Another bonus: the collapsible base makes the tray table easy to store when not in use.

Fixes

Top It Off Don't limit your choices; any sort of sturdy tray will work. You may want to consider something a bit offbeat and whimsical, such as these painted trays from the 1950s. Junk store finds, they are irrepressibly cheerful in a garden room. The bases are constructed from old bamboo fishing poles and wooden dowels.

Be Imaginative Place an old leather valise on a base to create a table that can double as extra storage space. The spare lines of the wooden base are tailored enough to allow the table to fit in with a variety of styles.

Set The Scene Tall backdrops of fabric or wood are good stand-ins for expensive artwork. They also give dressers and sideboards a little extra drama. Remember that these grand gestures work best if they're the same height as the door frames.

To mimic a fine Oriental screen, construct three tall wooden panels from stretcher strips purchased at an art supply store. With a staple gun, cover the panels with a tapestry-like fabric and hinge the panels together.

Or make a mirror rich in architectural detail. Search salvage yards for an old window frame. Paint or refinish it and have a mirror installed instead of glass.

Ottoman Empire

Large enough to use either as a coffee table or for extra seating, this project gives big returns but requires only basic sewing and carpentry skills.

Frame It Up

You will need two 30"-diameter rounds from ½"-thick plywood, usually available from home supply stores. You'll also need four 14" legs with brackets and screws from an upholstery shop and five ¼" x 2" bolts with washers and nuts.

Attach the four legs to a plywood round, spacing them equally around the perimeter and close to the edge. Drill four ¼" holes in the other round, equally spaced 7" from the edge. (These holes are for fastening the decorative buttons on top of the ottoman.)

Stack the rounds, carefully aligning the edges. Through both plywood rounds, drill five ¼" holes, equally spaced about 5" from the edges, being careful not to drill into the legs. Place a washer on each bolt and insert the bolts into the holes in the top round only; screw on the nuts to temporarily hold the bolts.

Undertake The Upholstery

You will need a round piece of 4"-thick medium-density foam 31" in diameter (cut at the fabric store); 45" square of bonded polyester batting; ¼" heavy-duty staples; four 1¼" button shells; four 1¼" flat buttons; heavy-duty thread; long upholstery needle; ½" shirring tape; and 3 yards of ⅝" cording.

The amount of fabric you will need depends on how full you want the skirt plus any extra material necessary to match design repeats. The ottoman shown here required 3½ yards of 54"-wide heavy brocade.

Position the foam over the top round of plywood, covering the bolt heads. Place the batting over the foam and cover it with a 45" square of the upholstery fabric. Pull the fabric tight and staple it to the bottom of the top round.

Cover the four button shells with leftover fabric. Using the upholstery needle, attach the heavy-duty thread to the back of the covered buttons. Then push the needle down through the fabric, batting, and foam, and into the ¼" holes drilled into the plywood round. Use the flat buttons to anchor the thread to the bottom of the round.

Make The Skirt

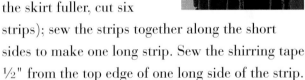

Cut four 17"-long strips across the width of the fabric (to make the skirt fuller, cut six strips); sew the strips together along the short sides to make one long strip. Sew the shirring tape ½" from the top edge of one long side of the strip.

Arrange the skirt around the edge of the bottom round and mark the depth of the hem; sew the two short ends of the skirt together and stitch the hem. Gather the skirt to fit the base, adjusting the gathers evenly; staple the skirt to the top of the bottom round.

Cut enough 2½"-wide strips on the bias of the fabric to total 100"; sew them together along the short edges to make one long strip. Cover cording with long strip to make welting. Staple welting to the top of the bottom round, overlapping ends. Unscrew the nuts from the bolts in the top round and bolt the two rounds together.

Quick Thinking

The flea market,
the craft-and-fabric shop,
the hardware store—wherever you
go this weekend, you'll find
the makings for your next
decorating project.

Golden Glow

It's curtains for dull tiebacks with this gold-plated technique. Coat a variety of silky flowers with a few layers of gold spray paint. After they're completely dry, hot-glue the flowers to purchased fabric tiebacks. Then all you have to do is secure your curtains with the gilded lilies.

Road Stories Pack up your troubles—not to mention your difficulty finding an end table. Stack old leather suitcases, found at flea markets and junk shops, for a table with built-in storage capabilities. Clean leather ones with saddle soap and shine them up with shoe polish, but remember that a few scratches and a number of shipping stickers add to their character.

Gothic Romance For a countrified headboard, look to whitewashed fence pickets. Buy enough Gothic-topped pickets—available at larger home-supply stores—to span the width of your bed and have them cut in lengths that will yield a symmetrical effect. Brace the headboard with stock lumber near the top and bottom of the pickets. Sand the headboard and paint it white. Bolt it to the bed frame and get ready for sweet dreams.

Bright Idea

They say almost anything can be wired and made into a lamp. A change from the usual ginger jars and bean pots: a baluster, one of the spindles from a dismantled staircase. Look for old ones at architectural salvage shops or find new ones at building supply stores. The long, curving shape of a baluster is a good foil for a classic parchment shade. For the best results, have the baluster drilled and the lamp electrified at a lamp store.

Cover Up Slipcover old pillows with a pinafore, an open-ended tube that fits around the pillow and ties on the sides. It's a pretty way to heighten contrasts of color and pattern. Make a pinafore out of summery madras with twill tape ties or use vintage tea towels secured with strips of grosgrain ribbon.

When Company's

Glad To See You Home is where the
heart is—yours and
everyone else's, thanks to
the **hospitality** of quick
decorating. Our clever seasonal
approaches will **secure** your
reputation as a great entertainer.
In the spring, **greet your guests** with
a natural welcome and beckon them inside with
the heavenly fragrance of
flowers. Come **summer,**
offer them the best
seat in the house, a

Coming

side chair
that you've
draped with
lace and tasseled with raffia. **Impress** them all with a
fall centerpiece arranged from little more than
nothing—**just a pair** of candlesticks and a few

bronzed blooms. By the time the winter
holidays arrive, you'll be on a roll. Trim the
tree, set the table, light
the candles, and answer

the door. The **house is ready**. And now,
so are you.

Spring

If the world is at your door, the least you can do is get ready.
The most fitting flourishes rely on the greenery that's
part and parcel of the season.

Herbal Essence To signal a casual dinner party, make a fresh and welcoming badge for the front door. From the herb garden, clip eight-inch stems of mint, rosemary, sage, oregano, thyme, or whatever is growing most abundantly. If you don't have a garden, purchase fresh herbs from the produce department of a grocery store.

Fasten a rubber band tightly around the herb stems. Wrap them in kraft paper and tie with twine. This quick-and-easy decoration lasts only a few hours without water, but you can then use the herbs in preparing your next meal.

Green Arches What could be more refreshing than flowers at your doorstep? Try flowers all around. This welcoming arch of fragrant mandevilla sweeps naturally from one side of the doorway to the other, creating the effect of a lush arbor.

It is supported by a framework of cut and dried kudzu vine ingeniously attached by hooks and wire to the door surround. If you don't want to wait for the flowers to grow into the kudzu, insert greenery and flowers in water picks for the short term—like the evening of a party. In winter, the kudzu could be a base for you to tuck in magnolia leaves, nandina branches, or evergreen boughs.

QUICK IDEA | **All Year Round** Christmas isn't the only time to adorn your door with a wreath. Many gardening catalogs offer both dried and fresh flower wreaths all year long. Or take advantage of seasonally available flowers with this idea: Buy a grapevine wreath from a crafts supply store and tie small apothecary bottles to it with raffia. Fill the bottles with water and insert fresh blooms.

Green Belt Cover a small wooden box with moss for a container as verdant as the plants it will hold. Fill it with glamorous houseplants, such as bromeliads and orchids, and you'll have a centerpiece to warm up brisk spring days.

You will need green sheet moss, a material that's available in a florist's shop or well-stocked crafts store. Select a wooden box or basket to serve as a base. Using a hot-glue gun and glue sticks, attach one piece of moss at a time, covering the exterior and lining the interior of the container.

Stick To It So that the box will not show through, glue small twigs to the edges of the box and over places where the pieces of moss meet.

Fill the box with assorted small plants, each in an individual container. Be sure to place a plastic saucer under each plant so that you'll be able to water the arrangement without disassembling it. Place a tall plant in a corner or in the center and cluster small ones around it.

If the moss begins to turn brown, mix a few drops of green food coloring with water and pour this mixture into a spray bottle. Spritz a few light coats onto the moss.

Wrap Stars Another easy twist is to wrap moss around small clay pots containing annuals and other bedding plants. Place each pot in a plastic saucer and then wrap a piece of moss around both the saucer and the pot. Use a length of string or raffia to hold the moss in place.

With the same idea, you can make miniature candle holders from little clay pots. Wrap each pot with a piece of moss and tie the moss in place. Insert a votive candle into each pot. Arrange the moss-covered plants and candle holders together on a tray for a centerpiece.

Splendor In The Grass

Real Easter egg grass— what could be more natural?

Line a basket with foil; then add small rocks and at least two inches of soil. Sow rye grass seeds generously and water with a spray bottle. Always keep the soil moist; spritz it a couple of times a day. Cover the basket with plastic wrap, punch a few holes in the wrap, and place out of direct sunlight. In about ten days, you should see grass blades emerging. Remove the plastic wrap. A week later, you'll have a "lawn" several inches tall.

Full Bloom

Force narcissus and hyacinth bulbs into glorious, sweet-smelling blossoms. Buy bulbs that are precooled or place them in the refrigerator for four to six weeks prior to planting.

To force narcissus, fill a shallow container with water and pebbles, positioning bulbs so that they are half buried. Add water. To force a hyacinth bulb, fill a hyacinth vase with water and set a bulb into the opening. Place the containers in a cool, dark location until roots and leaves develop; then move them to a sunny spot.

Pressing Matters A linen press is one of those old-fashioned ideas that will always make good sense. It's a pretty way to keep ironed cloth napkins and place mats wrinkle free.

To make one, you will need remnant wallpaper or heavy gift wrap, corrugated cardboard or mat board (available at arts-and-crafts stores), wide ribbon, and glue.

Cut two pieces of cardboard slightly bigger than your largest napkins. (If you are not sure what size napkins will be used in the press, a 19-inch square should accommodate most.) Next,

cut two pieces of wallpaper; each should be large enough to cover both sides of one piece of the cardboard. Wrap the individual pieces of cardboard completely, as if you were wrapping a gift. Glue the wallpaper in place and allow the glue to dry thoroughly.

Sandwich napkins and place mats between the two pieces of covered cardboard and secure with a generous length of ribbon. To keep the ribbon from raveling, cut the ends at an angle.

Store the press in a drawer or butler's pantry until the linens are needed.

Summer

When it's white-hot outside, keep your cool
with the right, light touch. After all,
the living's supposed to be easy.

Effortless Entertaining The no-fuss way to dress a table starts with a lace panel straight from a fabric store. Cover the table with it and you'll have a sheer base for summer party fare. Tabletop basics—a cool glass pitcher, vases, and white ceramic serving pieces—go atop spiky palm fronds (or whatever greenery you have around).

Shore Thing For everyday use, fold the lace panel in half and lay it diagonally across the table. Bunch the lace to create a more relaxed effect. You'll find these panels nearly foolproof to arrange; they have a woven border and, therefore, no hemming is required. Set the day's seaside finds on the cloth for a finishing touch.

Tasseled And Bedazzled Raffia has a simple, natural charm. These raffia tassels are a case in point. They're easy to make, and you can use them to jazz up the simplest of slipcovers: Arrange a lace panel in folds on a wooden chair and tie it in place with raffia strands edged with the tassels.

Quick Start Purchase a small roll of raffia at a crafts store and remove a dozen strands. Make a circle about six inches in diameter. Loop two or three more strands halfway through the circle and tie them in a knot. These loose strands will form the tassel tie.

Fine Finish Press the sides of the raffia circle together. Using several more raffia strands, wrap and bind the circle approximately one inch below the knot. Tie these strands in a knot and cut away the excess. To complete the tassel, cut the looped strands opposite the tassel tie.

A Tisket, A Tasket

Perch dried flowers around the rim of a basket. It's one way to make the flowers of summer last forever. You'll need: a light-colored, unfinished basket; acrylic paint in your choice of colors; sponge; clay pots in different sizes; and hot-glue gun and glue sticks. From a florist's shop or crafts store, purchase raffia, potpourri, and dried flowers.

Painterly Effects

Pour a small amount of paint onto a paper plate. (Mixing red oxide with burnt umber will duplicate the color of the clay pots.) Dampen a sponge with water and dab it into the paint; then sponge the paint onto the basket. Apply several light layers of color inside and out. Let dry.

Flower Power

Shorten each flower stem to six inches. Use the hot-glue gun to attach the flowers to the basket, overlapping the stems and arranging them close to the rim. Fill the basket with stacks of small clay pots turned at angles. Then add potpourri and more dried flowers. Complete the arrangement by tying on a few strands of raffia.

That Empty Feeling Containers are sometimes so decorative that they don't need to be filled with anything to make an arrangement that looks complete. Select several similar clay pots, pottery jars, baskets, or watering cans.

As these antique olive jars show, odd numbers always seem to work best. Experiment with the placement of the containers, turning them on their sides and adjusting their positions to take advantage of the changes in perspective.

Gold Fever Perhaps the best arrangements capture a moment in time within the growing season. In late summer, you'll treasure fruit-laden stalks and clusters of beans, along with tiny squash still on the vine. At the end of the season, when both flowers and vegetables are making their last grand show, it's a fine time to cut an entire stalk for the sake of a striking composition indoors.

Bouquets that combine dissimilar materials, such as sunflowers, spiky okra, and graceful branches of quince, are easier to manage if you have the right container. A tall vase with a narrow mouth is one of the easiest to use, because the small opening tends to do the arranging for you. Concentrate on collecting plants of different heights and shapes: some with upright lines, a mass to fill the center, and naturally trailing forms that will sweep down from the lip of the container.

Autumn

Maples blaze red, tulip poplars turn yellow, and oak leaves
drop a blanket of copper. It makes you want to bring all that color
into your home and live with it. Here's how you can.

Pick Of The Patch Pumpkin topiaries afford a fanciful composition for the front door. They're a stylish variation on the typical pumpkin on the porch.

For each one, you will need three pumpkins of graduated sizes, a large container, and about 15 feet of grapevine. If you can't get grapevine, honeysuckle or kudzu will work, too.

Although urns were used for these topiaries, large pots or baskets protected by a sheltered entry will work just as well. Before you head out to buy your pumpkins, measure the rim of the container. Make sure the largest pumpkin will perch atop the container without plopping down too far or balancing precariously. It's also a good idea to stack the pumpkins before buying them; look for a trio that balances in a straight line and is well matched.

If your stack is not as stable as you'd like, apply clear silicone sealant between the pumpkins for added security. If the skins aren't broken, they should last for a month.

Once you've arranged the pumpkins, loosely encircle them with loops of grapevine.

Easy Harvest One fast way to pick up some fall color is to stop by the local farmer's market. Load simple containers (such as the rough-hewn baskets often provided at the market) with vibrant fruits and vegetables. They may look great on the kitchen counter, but bring them into your living room and spread the bounty. Or scatter bright leaves across a tabletop. Protect them with a cover of sheer organdy and admire the colors as they show through the gauzy cloth.

The Naturals
Head outdoors to bask in an Indian summer afternoon. Set a special table where you can savor the scenery.

For a fast centerpiece, roll down the sides of a large paper bag and insert small pots of chrysanthemums; you can later transplant the flowers to the garden. Tuck loaves of French bread and a bottle of wine into your arrangement.

Squash, pumpkins, and other gourds are colorful accents that can bring the richness of autumn to your table. To complement them, use your simplest pottery, stainless cutlery, and fresh linens; serve bread on cutting boards.

Dry Season Grace your sideboard with a magnificent garland of dried leaves, flowers, and grasses. This also makes a handsome swag hung vertically on a wall or door, or as one of a pair on either side of a mantel.

Basic Form Cut a piece of 1-by-4-inch pine to the desired length and cover it with florist's foam using a hot-glue gun and glue sticks. Wrap the foam-covered board with chicken wire, stapling wire to the back. To protect furniture, cover the back with felt. Use the hot-glue gun to attach sheets of sphagnum moss to the bottom and sides.

Filling It Out Use a variety of natural materials. You can find them at a florist's shop or crafts store, or you can dry your own. Dried grasses, strawflowers, pods, hydrangea, cinnamon sticks, pinecones, and magnolia and oak leaves combine here for a lavish effect. Attach materials to florist's picks and insert them into the foam. Cluster stems to heighten the contrast of textures.

On A Pedestal Crown your candlesticks with flowers for a fast, effective centerpiece. The secret is an epergnette, an inexpensive adapter that's designed to sit atop a candlestick and turn it into a vase. Epergnettes are available from stores that sell floral supplies.

The epergnette contains a block of florist's foam, which should be removed and soaked in water. Once that's done, insert the stopper of the epergnette in the candlestick, replace the foam, and use an X of waterproof tape to secure it. Stick foliage into the foam, concealing the epergnette.

Cut short stems of flowers and insert them directly into the foam. Secure fruit to the foam with florist's picks.

If you use dried flowers and grasses (and dry florist's foam), your arrangement will last for several months.

Winter

Is there ever enough time during the holidays to do all that you want? Then deck the halls on the double.

Tremendous Trees A miniature forest of tabletop topiaries sets the stage for a dessert party. These rosemary, myrtle, and thyme plants have their foliage clipped into spheres.

Topiaries take time to grow, but, happily, you can purchase them fully grown at garden centers. Herbal topiaries require a lot of light. If you plan to keep one on a mantel or table longer than a few days, it's best to get two and alternate them.

All That Glitters The elegant tabletop covering is just a swirl of four yards of gold dress fabric and two yards of red damask. A plump knot tied in the gold fabric helps it fall gracefully over one edge of the table. Raw fabric edges are simply turned under, so no sewing is necessary.

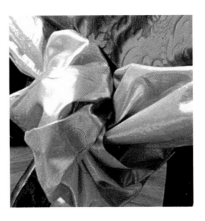

Nuts For Guests Pecans, almonds, cashews, and any other kind of nuts you'd care to name are traditional holiday treats. Since unshelled nuts look as good as they taste, set them out just about anywhere you want to offer a little welcome. Buy a bag of mixed nuts, pour them into a dish, toss in a nutcracker, and enjoy. Or specialize—purchase a bag of one type of nut and pour the contents into a large glass bowl. Either way, make the presentation special with a sprig of greenery or a twist of ribbon.

Take A Bow Beribboned decorations are a pretty way to signal the season. And what could be simpler? For a mantel arrangement with a Midas touch, tie gold and plaid ribbons onto brass candlesticks holding black beeswax candles. Another golden glow: bind bundles of cinnamon sticks with gold wire-edged ribbon and display them on a special silver salver.

Candlelight Vigil In a room with a beautiful tree and mounds of presents, it's best to keep the mantel decorations simple. Pillar candles in varying heights are perfect for that. To visually link them across the length of the mantel, twine them with gold ribbon and tinsel. Animate the arrangement with one special statue—like this sweet cherub—placed off center.

Season's Greenings The most festive tables often boast inspired collages. This one starts with a small container-grown evergreen tree. When it's kept moist, the tree can remain indoors for about ten days or two weeks and then be planted outside. The little tree keeps company with a trio of candles, a garden statue, and a porcelain compote filled with oranges for Christmas.

Run For It Cover your dining room table with a no-sew runner and you'll be all set for the holiday festivities. Fabric glue or a hot-glue gun and glue sticks attach the cording to the fabric, making any sewing unnecessary.

Count An Amount Measure the length of your table, add a yard, and purchase fabric equivalent to the total. Trim the fabric to the width you prefer. Cut each end so it tapers into a generous point. Press one inch under on all sides and use the fabric glue or hot-glue gun to secure the raw edges.

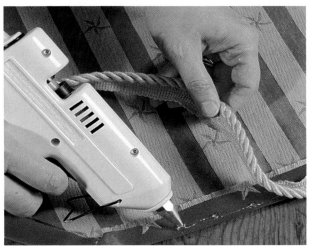

On The Border Measure around the outside edge of the runner, add six inches, and purchase cording or braid that is equivalent to this measurement. Glue the cording in place on the underside so that the decorative edging—and not the glued portion—is visible on the right side of the runner.

All That Glitters Quickly customize disposable plastic stemware and plates with an oil paint marker. Just use the marker to draw holiday motifs on the outside of the glasses and on the underside of the plates.

Baskets Of Blooms

Greet the new year with fresh flowers. At a time when weather is cold, daylight is short, and your home could use a lift, garden shops are filled with blooming plants. Let the variety inspire some wonderful floral combinations. Blend a half dozen different kinds of flowers together inside a splendid iron planter or basket.

No Muss, No Fuss

The key to achieving this look easily is to leave the plants inside their pots, so that each one can be removed and watered individually. When one plant begins to fade, you can quickly replace it without disturbing the entire arrangement.

Eternal Spring

When selecting the flowers for a planter, choose those that have not fully opened or else they will last only a few days. Once it's filled, keep the planter in bright sunlight to ensure that the flowers will bloom. Cool indoor temperatures of 60 to 65 degrees will help the arrangement last longer.

QUICK IDEA

Green Thumbs Up At the beginning of the year, greenhouses usually have kalanchoes, Christmas cacti, cyclamen, and amaryllis left over from the holidays. Most of these plants have weeks of blooms left. While flowers should dominate a planter arrangement, be sure to include a number of foliage plants to fill in gaps.

Quick Thinking

Let your guests know that you treasure
the pleasure of their company.
These fleet finishing touches offer
lots of ways to say
you're welcome.

The Graped Pumpkin A pumpkin becomes the
height of centerpiece sophistication when you
elevate it on an elegant silver compote. One
perched pumpkin is a stately centerpiece; a pair
of pumpkins in compotes makes beautiful
anchors for a buffet. For a natural topping,
secure a crown of red or green grapes to the soft
stem area with florist's picks.

Adorable Arrangement For a special shower or
luncheon, signal the festivities with a basket of flowers
on the door. A basket with one flat side will hug securely.
If your basket does not have a handle, add a length of dried
grapevine to hang it in place. Jars of water inside the basket
keep flowers fresh as long as possible, and cotton balls inside
the jars cushion the stems to eliminate splashing when the door
is opened and closed.

Nature's Way For summertime service, nothing tops a seashell. Nothing, that is, unless it's the salad course or any other part of the meal. Large shells, quickly collected at a beachside souvenir stand, are serendipitous stand-ins for casual serving pieces.

Here You Are The place card, a staple at formal dinners, is also a useful grace note for more casual get-togethers. This twig easel is a charming yet distinctly unfussy aid for directing your guests to their places. To make one, lash three twigs together with raffia to form a standing tripod. Tie a shorter stick to the front two legs and place the card on the little ledge.

Fruitful Efforts When is an apple more than an apple? When it's a candle holder, too. Ivory candles in an assortment of heights are inserted in shiny Granny Smith apples. Use an apple corer to cut holes; fill in, if necessary, with florist's putty for a snug fit. Tie taffeta ribbons into bows where the apples meet the candles. For more blooming beauty, hollow out a place in fruits and vegetables to hold a flower in a water pick.

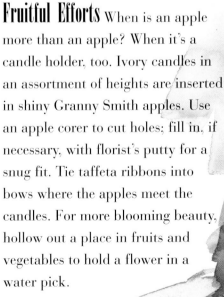

When You

So Tired Mundane mantel. Sluggish sofa. Pooped pillows. When it's **time** to liven things up, look to quick decorating. It **banishes boredom** with the greatest of ease. For a new look in **mere minutes**, start by shuffling things around. **Clear** off the mantel and

start over with a study in style. Then **rearrange** the furniture with some unexpected moves. Come on, bring those wicker chairs **inside** from the porch.

Want A Change

They'll **be perfect** around the dining room table. After that, **tie on** a slip-cover to give a sofa a new lease on life. Cover those old counter stools with a bright new fabric. **Exchange** your old pillows for some snappy new cushions. With quick decorating, you can do it all **on the double.** And you'll have nothing to lose but the blahs.

Warm Up The Mantel

It's almost always a focal point.
Give it a different arrangement
and make the whole room
seem new.

Service Plates When a room has as many strong
features as this one—a cathedral ceiling, floor-
length windows, bright fabrics, and colorful artwork—only the simplest adornment is needed for
the great white mantel. Five inexpensive wooden
plates, purchased at an import store, make a
fresh and uncomplicated grouping. Acrylic stands
clearly provide the necessary support. The plates
are set asymmetrically on the mantel and arrayed
in a way that shows off their natural grain.

Balanced View Symmetry, another way to pull a mantel together, is easy to achieve because it takes much of the guesswork out of decorative display.

Start with a central element like the carriage clock that's set in front of the large painting. Then work from the center out, putting in pairs of items.

Expect to use trial and error. As you add sets of objects, stop to see if the arrangement looks pleasing. No one element should overpower the rest. For that reason, don't hesitate to split things up—the leather-bound books above show how effective that can be.

On Reflection A mirror alone above a mantelpiece can look cold and stark. But a gallery of framed photographs along the base of the mirror cozies up the setting and gives the eye something new to look at. To heighten the sense of liveliness, some of the frames are elevated on small books and everything is candle lit.

Close Counts Don't think you must have two of everything to pull off an effective arrangement. Although some repetition is essential, you needn't be limited to the predictable. Insert items that are similarly sized but not exactly alike; they'll still balance. That's why the "vase" of painted flowers works with the rabbit print.

Simple Addition

Give a plain fireplace a mantel and in return you'll gain prominent display space for some of your personal treasures.

To determine the size of your mantel, consider both the scale of the fireplace and the accessories you plan to use. The cost of the project will depend on your needs.

A carpenter constructed the pair of white mantel shelves by embellishing crown molding from the hardware store. (Similar shelves are available from home design catalogs.) Because

the lines are simple and classic, these shelves would complement rooms in many styles.

Another versatile mantel: setting a polished glass shelf atop two gilded brackets. Because the glass is heavy—this half-inch-thick piece weighs about 30 pounds—screw the brackets directly into wall studs for best support. For extra security, install the brackets with molly bolts or toggle bolts. To determine the length of the shelf, measure the space between brackets and add an eight-inch overhang.

Change Of Context

You Put It Where? Use your furniture in new and different ways to change the look of a room—you don't have to spend lots of money for great results. Instead of having a complete set of matching chairs at a table, mix in a wicker settee and chairs from the porch. Then just let your imagination guide you to places for other pieces. You might not think of placing a bureau in a bath, but when you consider the space you gain for towels and toiletries, it makes perfect sense.

Change Of Cover

For fast freshness, consider restyling with slipcovers.
This popular design solution offers both style and economy.

New Clothes Slipcovers have always been a prime way to reflect changes in the seasons. But as an alternative to reupholstering, slipcovers are a great idea year-round. For one thing, the cost of having your slipcovers made is roughly half the cost of upholstering. (Ask at fabric stores for the names of slipcover makers.) For another, their soft fabrics can deliver dressmaker details such as pockets, shirring, and pleating that are difficult to achieve with stiff upholstery materials.

Detailing on slipcovers can also restyle or update furniture without the expense of actually rebuilding it. You can completely change the character of a contemporary sofa, for example, by covering it in floral chintz fashioned with layers of ruffles and fringe.

Slipcovers are also invaluable for pulling unmatched pieces together. You can cover a vintage chair and a spare ottoman—like the pair shown here—in the same fabric, easily creating an attractive and well-coordinated ensemble.

Slipcases New slipcovers let you change the feel of a room instantly. With softly fitted floral fabric you can relax the mood; while a tone-on-tone stripe quickly adds sophistication.

Natural-fiber fabrics like cotton or linen generally work better than synthetics for slipcovers because they are more supple. Drapery fabrics are superior to upholstery materials, which tend to be heavy and unyielding. You can expect thick cottons and linens, particularly in dark colors or patterns, to wear well under heavy use.

To avoid eventual shrinkage, wash or dry-clean the fabric before having the slipcovers made. Get specific information on fabric care from the shop where you purchase the yardage. Custom-made slipcovers trimmed with fringe, braid, or tassels usually should be dry-cleaned, but some cottons and blends are washable—a plus if you have young children or pets.

If you do have machine-washable slipcovers, simply launder them and dry on a low setting; then put them on the furniture while still slightly damp. The wrinkles will fall out.

French Dressing A wing chair exchanges Colonial styling for Gallic flair when it dons a slipcover of blue-and-white French toile. This printed fabric, which was first fashionable during the eighteenth century, is enjoying renewed popularity. Bows add a romantic detail as they tie up the back of the chair; they're a soft alternative to snaps or zippers.

Skirting The Issue

A side chair takes on a brand-new identity with a plaid fabric slipcover whose gathered skirt extends to the floor. You can slipcover an entire set of dining room chairs or just the ones at the head and foot of the table. Slipcovering an odd wooden chair from the attic is an imaginative way to furnish a room and add a dash of color.

Pleased To Seat You In just a few hours, you can re-cover barstools or chair seats with new fabric. Measure one seat, adding six inches to both length and width. Purchase this amount for each chair. If your fabric has a design that needs to be centered, you will need more total yardage.

Cut the fabric for each seat cover to the measured dimensions. Center the fabric on the seat and turn the fabric and seat right side down. Holding the fabric taut, use a staple gun to attach each side at the center back. Then staple from the center to the corners, easing in the fullness at the corners. After the fabric is securely attached on all sides, reattach the seat to its frame.

Fabric Infatuation Assembling a cohesive design scheme is easy when you choose fabrics from a manufacturer's coordinated collection. These assortments are available in designs to suit any room. Sometimes called design groups, they often include wallpaper and borders in addition to fabrics and trimmings. And most collections come in a variety of color schemes.

In selecting patterns from a collection, consider how they'll be used. Scale is important, so reserve large patterns for big projects such as curtains or a sofa. Save the smallest designs for pillows and fabric blinds.

To make the most accurate judgments, take home samples of fabrics and trims. Look at them in natural light alongside your own furniture and accessories.

Master Of Disguises

The round skirted table, that decorating perennial, is a versatile and inexpensive standby. These new variations cleverly enhance the old practicality.

Hide And Seek A cardboard barrel makes a great storage place for ornaments, seasonal decorations, or other items you rarely need. Even better, a barrel can quickly become a useful piece of furniture. Just take a standard storage barrel (purchased at a home-supply store or moving company) and pack your items in it. Then top it with a 28-inch round of plywood.

Drape the plywood with a linen tablecloth, and you instantly have a skirted table. A handkerchief effect like this one is easily achieved by adding a square overlay of coordinating fabric. You can place this table beside a chair or

sofa, or on its own to fill an empty corner.

Change the skirts and overskirts on any table with each new season or occasion. Fabric selection depends on how the table is going to be used. If the skirt will cover a dining table, choose a tightly woven, washable fabric for the easiest upkeep. For a table where you'll display family photographs, books, or a collection of wooden boxes, select a fabric that drapes well but still has body.

An inside tip: Place an old quilt or blanket over the table before you put the fabric on. The thick underlayer will automatically make the top cloth look richer and more substantial.

QUICK IDEA | **Round And Round** Call on some basic geometric skills to make sure your circular cloth is the proper size. To determine the diameter of the circle of fabric you'll need, measure the diameter of the tabletop. Then add twice the measurement from the top to the floor and include an allowance for the hem. This formula works for a classic look. If you prefer the luxurious effect of a cloth puddling on the floor, add another 12 to 18 inches.

Pillows Talk

Casual or formal? Answer the question
just by swapping the pillows on your sofa.
Then change your mind again anytime you want.

The Cushy Life For a dressy effect, pillows made from cut velvet, tapestry, and a fragment of an Aubusson rug nestle on a tailored white sofa. For a more informal look on the same sofa, chintz pillows plumply fill in.

Whatever your design style, there are a number of tried-and-true ways to coax more life from your pillows. For starters, use different but compatible fabrics on each side. A cotton check or stripe suits a flowered chintz; pair velvet with needlepoint or tapestry.

Incorporate small bits of lace, tapestry, or needlepoint into your design by sewing the fragments onto larger pieces of velvet. For maximum effect, apply trim around the edges of finished pillows.

You can also vary the look with different sizes. Choose pillows in 18-inch squares rather than the more common 15-inch squares. The extra heft denotes luxury, while the extra cost is negligible.

No-Hassle Hassocks

Ottomans are the chameleons of decorating. You can change their look in a trice. It's simplicity itself to cover an ottoman with a rug—a fine kilim, sewn or tucked under to secure, assures success.

For a slightly more ambitious redo, transform an old rattan stool into an up-to-date ottoman using fabric and a pair of round cushions. This particular stool is covered with recycled drapery material. Alternatively, you could use inexpensive fabric or a small tablecloth.

To make this no-sew project: Place the cushions on top of the stool. Secure the cushions to the stool using ribbon, twine, sewing tape, or anything thin enough not to show through the fabric. Tie secure knots under the stool. Measure from the center of the top cushion to the floor, adding a few extra inches for a puddling effect.

Spread the fabric on the floor. Mark the center with chalk; around that point, mark your cushion-to-floor measurement, making a circle. Cut out the fabric circle. To cover the raw edges, use a hot-glue gun and glue sticks to apply fringe or trim.

Place the skirt on the stool. Arrange the fabric and tie it in place with twine. Knot decorative cording—with tasseled ends, if desired—to camouflage the twine.

Quick Thinking

Turn dull befores into
some happily ever afters when
you learn to recast the ordinary.
With extraordinary results,
you'll never be tired of
your rooms again.

Pattern Logic

Liven up a plain wall
with the drama of tapestry—
this simple little-sew project
makes the most of the fabric's
intricate motifs. "Hem" all sides of a length of
tapestry with fusible web; with heavy thread,
stitch a pocket at the top big enough to accommodate a wooden drapery rod. Hang the rod on
the wall and loop tassels and cording around the
top of the fabric for a final fillip.

Paper Chase Plain paper lampshades, cheap and
serviceable, can be gussied up in a hurry with details
that complement any design style. For a contemporary
turn, use a craft knife to cut "windows" in a regular
pattern around the shade. To get a rustic effect,
use a hole punch to perforate a shade with a crown of
holes; run rawhide through the holes and secure the ends in a
knot. Or cross-stitch the top and bottom of a perforated shade with strips of raffia.

Porcelain Complexion

The place for china, whether inherited or collected, is out of the china closet. Mismatched cups and pots, united by a floral theme, serve up a tasty new look on a wide mantel.

Hang In There

A porcelain tieback hook is an exemplary hanger for a moiré ribbon-bound botanical print. Old hooks like this, found at antiques shops and secondhand stores, are a refreshing way to hang old-fashioned prints and engravings. New wrought-iron tieback hooks (and lengths of tailored cording) would offer a sculptural support for a collection of architectural prints or black-and-white photographs.

Pluperfect Pillows

You know what a scarf can do for a basic dress; now see what it can do to dress up your old pillows—with no sewing, cutting, or gluing needed. Set a pillow diagonally on a square scarf; pull all corners of the scarf to the center of the pillow and secure them with a rubber band. Spread the ends in a neat, symmetrical arrangement or tuck the ends to form a rosette.

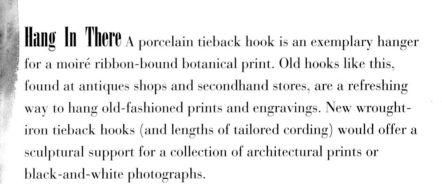

Index

Acknowledgments

Many individuals have given generously of their time and talent in the production of *SOUTHERN LIVING Quick Decorating*. We extend special thanks to the many homeowners around the South who have welcomed *Southern Living* editors and photographers into their homes. They include Suzanne and Robert Chesnut, Philip Morris, Cathy and Paul Chapman, Kreis and Sandy Beall, George-Ann and Boone Knox, Pat and Wayne Terry Lamar, Angelyn and Ken Lewis, Katie Stoddard, Eleanor and Jim Thomason, Dolly and Jim Walker, and Dede and Greg Wood.

Our contacts in the design community are an invaluable source of ideas and inspiration. Among the architects and designers whose work is pictured on these pages are: Claudia Aquino, Atlanta; Ballard Designs, Atlanta; Ann Carter, Jackson, Mississippi; Donna Cunningham, Houston; Roy Dollar, Birmingham; Jenny Fitch, Pittsboro, North Carolina; Marjorie H. Johnston, Birmingham; Carter Kay, Atlanta; Carolyn Malone, Atlanta; Shane Meder, Atlanta; Maureen Miller, Lake Charles, Louisiana; Warner Moore, Memphis; Joetta Moulden, Houston; Thomas Pope, Key West; Carrie Raeburn, Coffee Springs, Alabama; Naomi Thomason, Birmingham; Scott Tichenor, Louisville, Kentucky; and Pamela Wright, Arlington, Virginia.

This book is the result of a collaborative effort on the part of many staff members at *Southern Living*. Editor John Floyd, Operations and Publications Manager Bill McDougald, and Eleanor Griffin, Executive Editor for Homes and Gardens, were always encouraging and insightful as they suggested innovative approaches to decorating. The Homes staff, including Homes Editor Linda Hallam, Building Editor Louis Joyner, and Associate Interiors Editor Mary McWilliams, originated many of the story ideas. They also traveled extensively, locating homes to photograph and information to include. Linda Askey, Associate Garden Editor, and Leslie Byars, Photo Stylist, also contributed. Katherine Pearson, former Executive Editor, worked on the concept and helped keep it focused. Several former staffers, including Carole Engle-Avriett, Deborah Hastings, and Todd A. Steadman, also contributed.

The *Southern Living* photographers have enriched nearly every page of the book. They include: Van Chaplin, Cheryl Dalton, Tina Evans, Sylvia Martin, Art Meripol, Emily Minton, John O'Hagan, Howard L. Puckett, and Charles Walton IV. The work of former *Southern Living* photographer Colleen Duffley is also included. Special thanks go to Catherine Perry, who coordinated photo research.